Starland

Starland

Poems by
Brenda Sciberras

TURNSTONE PRESS

Starland
copyright © Brenda Sciberras 2018

Turnstone Press
Artspace Building
206-100 Arthur Street
Winnipeg, MB
R3B 1H3 Canada
www.TurnstonePress.com

MIX
Paper from
responsible sources
FSC
www.fsc.org
FSC® C004071

Turnstone Press gratefully acknowledges the assistance of the Canada
Council for the Arts, the Manitoba Arts Council, the Government of
Canada, and the Province of Manitoba through the Book Publishing Tax
Credit and the Book Publisher Marketing Assistance Program.

Printed and bound in Canada.

Library and Archives Canada Cataloguing in Publication

Sciberras, Brenda, 1958-, author
    Starland / Brenda Sciberras.

Poems.
Issued in print and electronic formats.
ISBN 978-0-88801-637-9 (softcover).--ISBN 978-0-88801-638-6
(EPUB).--ISBN 978-0-88801-639-3 (Kindle).--ISBN 978-0-88801-640-9
(PDF)

    I. Title.
PS8637.C597S73 2018   C811'.6   C2018-901372-9
                                                  C2018-901373-7

MANITOBA ARTS COUNCIL
CONSEIL DES ARTS DU MANITOBA

Canada Council   Conseil des arts
for the Arts   du Canada

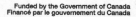

Funded by the Government of Canada
Financé par le gouvernement du Canada   Canada   Manitoba

To my Mother, Stella
for everything

I am grateful to my Father for the movies, the music,
and the memories

Contents

~

~

~

~

Starland

There is one glory of the sun,
and another glory of the moon,
and another glory of the stars:
for one star differeth from
another star in glory.

—1 Corinthians 15:41

Stars

A star begins its career

             as a protostar

  &

            the stages to stardom are long

The smallest of stars

           have lengthier lives

     unless

           they commit suicide

A celestial sphere

      of
           Inflated egos
              Alcoholism
                 Drug addiction

Life – span

           depends

              on the masses

&

the stars'

luminosity

Left to their own

devices

they collapse

under their own weight

Rapid & violent

nothing can stop them

even those who cluster

around

become a stellar remnant

burn out

sink

into a black

hole

The silence of a falling star
Lights up a purple sky
And as I wonder where you are
I'm so lonesome I could cry.
                                    —Hank Williams

Lonesome

I'm so lonesome I could cry.
We used to email, we used to call,
Now it seems there's no will to try.

Yes, we're Facebook friends, by & by.
You know it's all the rage; writing on one's wall.
I'm so lonesome I could cry.

Sometimes you "Like" what I post… I can't lie,
Might manage an emoji, usually nothing at all.
Now it seems there's no will to try.

They say the Internet keeps friends tied;
I don't believe that to be true.
I'm so lonesome I could cry.

All your posts are of happy times. Why?
Have you no thoughts that are blue?
Now it seems there's no will to try.

Lately, texts are all I get… I say this with a sigh.
& the phone never rings. Hell, I could have died.
I'm so lonesome I could cry.
Now it seems there's no will to try.

Cadillac

Last night I dreamed
I was ridin' in Hank Williams'
'52 robin's egg blue Cadillac.

All the windows rolled down
heat of the day wavin' us by
a grey day, not a smear of sunshine.

Hank was wearin' his white Stetson
his scuffed boots well worn
but still holdin' a shine.

His knees driftin' up real high
long bony fingers of his large hands
restin' on his caps.

I started just talkin' about poetry.
He said, *I ain't read any poetry
only comic books.*

He had a smirk & a laugh
I thought I'd never see nor hear again.
He lit a smoke, then took a swig from his silver flask.

So, I asked Ol' Hank, why do you write such sad songs?
He tugged at his Adam's apple and replied
Aw hell I reckon the world's just a sad sad place
& I couldn't deny that.

He asked what I was writin' & if it was sad too?
Well, I said, my happy poem's 'bout a dead dog.
That made him chuckle, passin' me his flask, sayin'
Honey, you need this half as much as I do.

Ballad of Hank Williams

From shoe rag to steel guitar
I was just a skinny hillbilly kid
but my singin' would make me a big country star
There'll never be another like Ol' Hank

Readin' comic books all the time
sellin' peanuts and sandwiches
just to make a dime
There'll never be another like Ol' Hank

At six I was sayin', I wish I had a dad!
by eleven I was drinkin' whisky from a mason jar
strummin' a cheap guitar, yodelin', and feelin' sad
There'll never be another like Ol' Hank

I knew I oughta be in school
but I was playin' with guns and fishin' in the creek
I'm *The Singing Kid* and nobody's fool
There'll never be another like Ol' Hank

Honky Tonks and Hayrides I'd soon master
Ol' Hank here knew what he was doin'
writin' songs, singin', drinkin', and screwin' came after
There'll never be another like Ol' Hank

From birth I had this pain in my back that needed lookin' after
still I kept singin' those tremors and wobbles
hid the pain with booze, pills, and young girls' laughter
There'll never be another like Ol' Hank

Now, I'm smitten with a pretty gal named Audrey
I bought a big white hat and a blue Cadillac
got high hopes of makin' the Grand Ole Opry
There'll never be another like Ol' Hank

Knee-bent and yodelin', I kept moanin' out the blues
my band's called the *Drifting Cowboys*
ya know there's no other life I'd choose
There'll never be another like Ol' Hank

Sellin' records, breakin' bottles, breakin' hearts
writin' songs on scraps of paper and cuffs of my shirt
Billboard magazine says I'm a superstar
There'll never be another like Ol' Hank

I'm poppin' plenty of pills, just to kill the pain
Audrey and me are fightin', all the time
sometimes I ask, is this the price of fame?
There'll never be another like Ol' Hank

So, I summons *Luke the Drifter*
'cause he'll say the things I just can't
money flows like liquor and Audrey sure likes all the glitter
There'll never be another like Ol' Hank

When I hear that lonesome whistle, I get to feelin' blue
they call me a humble poet, but I don't know
still common folk believe what I say is genuine and true
There'll never be another like Ol' Hank

Gosh that Audrey has a cold cold heart
she's cruel as can be when I go see Bocephus, my baby boy
you know, Mama never liked her, from the very start
There'll never be another like Ol' Hank

So, I've got the lovesick blues, 'cause Audrey's filed for divorce
on the rebound weddin' bells ring for me and Billie Jean
a pretty little thing who's wearin' my ring of course
There'll never be another like Ol' Hank

In West Virginia it's a cold and stormy night
still, we're drivin' down that lost highway tryin' to get to the next gig
I hear Jesus callin' and I say to my driver, *I saw the light*
There'll never be another like Ol' Hank

Now, I lie in a silver casket, my favourite boots cradle my feet
they bury my body back in old Montgomery
I leave behind a not-yet-born baby girl I'll never meet
There'll never be another like Ol' Hank

I'm the kid some said would never amount to nothin'
at my funeral they sang *When God Comes and Gathers His Jewels*
thousands line the street, 'cause they were mournin'
There'll never be another like Ol' Hank

Tears Dry

Today I cried for you on my hardwood floor.
You said you were trouble,
that you were no good,
but you cheated yourself,
carved initials in your arm,
a tattooed rebel, razors & ribs.
Hovering between Motown & Sinatra,
The Ronettes & Vaughan,
your vintage voice often a slur.
The ghost of jazz dancing a cappella
to your Amy antics.
& I'll miss you, body & soul.

Today I cried for you on my hardwood floor.
But, let's be frank, when I first saw you
I took you for a freak. That beehive hairdo
& Cleopatra eyes, your body a flute.
Daddy's Girl, needled on your arm,
a radical Virgo, pendula of chaos
you rise like smoke.
& the paps snap shots,
tabloids track you toiling
with your own grandeur,
struggling against futile odds,
bedraggled, you send them clamouring.

Today I cried for you on my hardwood floor.
White wine & Smirnoff replace powder & puff
& the doomsayers drink your drama,
swallow you back to black,
turn your horseshoe upside down,
stop   the applause,
silence   the metropolis of your retro soul.
But, your daddy thought you were fine.
rehab no no no, your day has come,
Club Forever Twenty-Seven, fate resigned.
Now, so far away, eternal bird & butterfly,
you know no regrets.

Amy

reclaim
musician

portrait of the artist

truest

jazz singer

legacy

creative process
artistic journey

the diary
she writes

becomes a poem
becomes lyrics

layers
songs

Life Ain't Easy for a Spider Named Johnny Cash
(*The Guardian* Feb. 5, 2016)

In the Sierra Nevada mountains
under the light of the moon
there's a black tarantula crawling
scaling the wall of Folsom Prison
just to keep a close watch
over inmates locked
where time keeps draggin' on
those deviant souls
alone when each day is through
pray for redemption
with mutiny on their minds

Johnny Cash sang to those killers
rapists & robbers too
that man in black
with his mournful voice
could hum their cares away
'cause under their steel sky
they hadn't seen the sun
shine since I don't know when
rifle-barrelled walls
outside a river wide
like a ring of fire
keepin' them penned up inside

Now, this black-clad specimen
is just trying to break in
with the jingle of the guards
on gunwalks above
shooting down at any
thing that moves
well life ain't easy
for a spider named Johnny Cash
they'd just as soon
shoot him
just to watch him die

Serious Moonlight

I had forgotten
    how beautiful
        his lyrics

That I had danced
    like a rebel
        believed he was my hero

And the crowd
    toking fans ready
        to blow their minds

On that warm
    autumn night
        when the stars sang

Not knowing that
    what we had witnessed
        would transcend our youth

Over the years
    I'd forgotten his ethereal presence
        here on earth

But, now the news
    has just come over
        that he's gone

No more Bowie
   no more encores
      into my golden years

And the stars
   look very different
      for me tonight

Desire Diner
(for Jann Arden)

I have an appetite for writing
a thirst for composition
I go looking for it
want to cook up a poem
like a French chef—al dente

Whip up an ode to a friend
a wonderdrug for one who's sick
I want to mix metaphors, stir in similes
pare down the obscurities
that leave it hanging by a thread
Just like a good mother
I want to nurture my poem
fold in aromatic imagery

There is time for mercy
in this creative process
the poet only needs to caramelize an idea
Yet, an interlude I've become
solidified in images of serving
Jann Arden's meatloaf
on a plate forest green with envy
smothered in gravy, parsley garnished

Sipping latte over conversations
of words & wonder
I think never mind
You are my mulled muse
a matriarch of music
your beat dissolves my resolve
but I will deny being a groupie
savour the labyrinth of desire
digesting in me

Popstar

We jump on your bandwagon
ride your teen idol tube
your *baby* voice upstaging all.
You give teens a *purpose*
beauty & a beat, sing, *love yourself.*

We brag your patronage
& when things go *all bad*, we bail.
It makes *no sense*.
You've had your share of growing
pains & parties.

Learn from your mistakes
that's *all that matters*.
I *believe* you're wiser
more confident
& everything will *be alright.*

Naysayers say
slights & slurs
the media pounces
(platinum album aside).
It's not too late to say sorry.

Like they've never had a *bad day*!
What do you mean? Deportation!
You've been *all around the world*
our true Canadian *boyfriend*, we'll
never let you go—
but stop the train wreck!

Sorry Biebs.

Stardust

                            an artist
                just died
                            work   created becomes
                currency
fans
cluster
last long after   tributes disappear
                             Bowie

                             Jim Morrison
Elvis Presley
                    Bob Marley
            Kurt Cobain

                                            Amy Winehouse
                             Janis Joplin
nothing
        will   fade

            Michael Jackson
                    Immortal
                                            each
                piece of art   more valuable
                        the artist who made it is gone
                    interest never dies
                                You have to
stay true to the artist
            fans are keeping
                    memorials   across the world
                                all welcome
                                        soon after
brought back to life

when wish is merest touch I bend
like her whose curve is heaven over earth
and love beneath me far and far
makes of my flesh a miracle of stars

"Seeds and Stars"
The Shadow-Maker
—Gwendolyn MacEwen

Story of a Book

tattered & worn
wrinkled leaves
coffee ringed
pages torn
some missing
spine broken
words scribbled
in margins in pencil
or red ink
some words crossed out
some words circled
arrows & lines
its rough texture
faded façade
this book
its story
is not enough
now overlooked
time after time
because of age
and appearance
but words are waiting
prose & poem
wanting to be pulled
from the shelf
fondled by fingers
read out loud

Throwback

Gone are the textbooks
& typewriters of the past
classroom blackboards
have all been taken down
the library circulates laptops
Shakespeare's sonnets sit
on the shelf wanting to be read
there's no study of Dickens or Keats
Austen or Bronte
Plath & her poetry
long forgotten for a lyric of a song
the dress code has died too
never mind that navy tunic
from my girlhood past
on to denim & spandex
slippers not shoes
baseball hats not thinking caps
away with dresses & freshly pressed slacks
on with throwback Thursday
let's all wear plaid

Pansies for Sylvia

pressing purple
between worn pages
Plath's parting
poems.

predicting her final
resting place
beneath paper
thin lines
on frowning faces

as if
they knew
how precious
were her words.

What Else Can We Do

In the cold insulated winter
locked inside
frost on the pane
furnace & fire absolute
wool socks & flannel shirts
a cup of tea
with a shot or two of whiskey

what else can we do
but write poetry
held up here in these walls
wind & white gusting outside
we read Cohen,
Crozier, or Cooley
depending on our mood

Kroetsch's *Seed Catalogue*
reminding us of a spring to come
of colour & the smell of earth
what else can we do
but find a metaphor
that warms us

Yesterday's News

In ten maybe twenty years
there will be no such thing
as a daily newspaper
no pages to flip or fold
no crossword to scribble
no movie section
to circle or rip out
no book reviews
no paper delivery guy or gal
no subscription
to cancel for summer vacation
it's all yesterday's news
the scandals & gossip
well that's hardly news at all!
paper copies only a memory
our news we'll read
with the click of a mouse
a slight scroll of the hand
in twenty words or less
grammar deleted
from our vocabulary
no more smell of ink
blackened fingertips
or coffee smudge to read around
where will the archives go
to that cloud in the sky?

EXTRA, EXTRA read all about it!
can't say no news is good news

After Leonard Cohen's "How to Speak Poetry"

Take the word star. To use the word it is not necessary to think
bright or twinkling. It's not necessary to have hit your head to
see them. It's not necessary to look upward to the heavens. The
word star does not necessarily mean it's above us. Stars could
be in a theatre or café. You may walk past a star on the street &
you might not even notice. It could be on a page. There's a star
in *The Little Prince*. Everyone knows the Bible is scattered with
stars. This poem is nothing but information. There are more
stars in the sky than people on earth. When man destroys
the earth will he destroy the stars too? Can a star start a war?
When I speak of a star you know I'm not speaking of the
sparkling kind as some stars can be quite dull. But when they
get all fired up who knows. Did you know that there are even
best famous star poems? When I was a little girl I heard the
song *A Thousand Stars* on the radio & I wanted to count them.
Jiminy Cricket sings, *When You Wish Upon a Star*. If a cricket
can sing about stars I can write a poem about them.

In Memoriam

I said to Hank Williams, "How lonely does it get?"
Hank Williams hasn't answered yet,
but I hear him coughing all night long,
a hundred floors above me in the tower of song.

"The Tower of Song"   —Leonard Cohen

You pondered your own impending death
your poems and songs reflect this candidness
your time on this earthly plane was running out
you thought of others who'd gone to the Great Beyond
wondering if you'd meet them with the angels above
if you'd be afraid or filled with regret
like Ol' Hank, you always seemed older than your years
hid inside that three-piece suit, fedora resting on top
smooth talk another pretty lady, smoke another cigarette
I said to Hank Williams, "How lonely does it get?"

Sometimes you'd speak to the dead, out loud or in your head
those conversations a muse for a poem or lyrics for a song
you explored mortality, toyed with your demise
sat in the third-row pew, prayer book in hand
Montreal your refuge when you felt the world had gone mad
I know your artist life was a bit like playing Russian Roulette
over the years, you did try to settle down and make a change
retreated to a monastery seeking answers
wrote questions on the wall in the Hebrew Aleph Bet
Hank Williams hasn't answered yet,

You thought you weren't finished
had songs yet to sing
but in your heart, you felt like it might be closing time
just as Ol' Hank who knew his last days were upon him
he died much younger than you, yet I know
you couldn't help dream of him riding in that blue Cadillac
you shared the gift of voice, I still hear you singing long after
        you've gone
Hallelujah and *I Saw the Light*, your mantras
you both burnt bridges & I'm not one to judge
I know you weren't scared to die, you live in the *Tower of Song*
but I hear him coughing all night long,

All this time Hank's up there singing & playing his guitar
while you've been writing poems & lyrics here like a star
the time has passed ever so quickly
eighty-two frail pages from an aged book
turning like tunes on an old phonograph record
You Want It Darker was your swan song
& I'm sure you're thankful you got to play *The Favourite Game*
now, in the synagogue the cantor & choir sang
'cause Marianne was waiting far too long
a hundred floors above me in the tower of song.

All the world's a stage,
And all the men and women merely players…

—Shakespeare, *As You Like It*, Act II, Scene vii

Saturday Matinee

We walk down Main up to Logan
my hand in his colossal palm.

My Father comforts
me with just his smile.

Big Brother walks on ahead
denying any need. He's eleven.

We enter the Starland vestibule.
My Father pulls change from his pocket,

a buck & a half for the three tickets, two
bits each for my brother & me. A bargain

for this Saturday matinee, a double feature.
King Kong & *Son of Kong.*

The theatre's large paint-peeled doors creak
open to a sculpted ceiling, faded & frayed

carpet. Maroon threadbare seats give off
a musty odour, a strange sour smell.

The popcorn has an old taste & the Nibs aren't soft.
We sit backs against the wall, my Father

in the middle, not so we don't fight, he says,
but so he can guard us with his watchful eyes.

I'm not sure who he is watching or why
but I sense that he should.

Lights dim. The curtain rises.
The overture begins.

Starland

Starland is where we mortals go
to sit upon old velvet seats crusted
with cum, eat bags of rancid popcorn
dream of being rescued from Brontë by Kong
bitten on the box by Dracula, buriedalive
like the Mummy or scream along
with the Japanese, as Godzilla
crushes their running children.

Starland is where we mortals wish
to be as chinadolldelicate as Fay Wray.
As wonderlustful with twinkling
bigbrowneyes, pucker our cherry
lips & kiss her leading man
the prick from his own neverneverland
dead already from drugs & drink
women & want, who materialized
in the shadows of a wideanglelens.

Starland is where nothingisasitseems
only illusionopaque paintedonglass
mounted in front of a camera
cardboard cutouts & miniature projection
an eternal lost world
happyeverafter or terrified to death
life in focus or OUT. That's why we're
sitting in the Starland darkened watching
the credits roll by.

Sani sita malem ati-kow dia malem ma pakeno
I will give six women like this for your woman of gold

Media Illusions

What if Kong was white—an albino
What if his dream girl was black
He the symbol of purity & chastity
Untarnished by society's injustices
Free from the tall, dark, & handsome profile

What if Ann looked into Kong's deep
Pink eyes and saw only her reflection
Not the lustful seductive dark we are drawn to
Would we sympathise with his longing, his desire
To get the 'girl.' Would Kong seem
As threatening beating a broad white chest

What if Ann didn't wear that blonde wig
The one with ringlets flowing down her shoulders
What if her opaque translucent skin
Were as midnight dark as our original ape
Her short black curls tightly embracing her round face
Give her fifty more pounds of flesh & subtract
That hourglass figure, add a white veil of fog
& your 'woman of gold' becomes the perfect bride
'The scream that shook the world' an octave or two lower

What if Ann dropped her clothes, naked as the ape
Kong would clearly see what he was getting
No false illusions to reckon with, no sheer dress to peel away
His massive fingers exploring her thighs & bosom
Would he want to seduce Ann, screw her brains out
Or see her as dark & evil, forget his sexual appetite
Just go ahead & eat her in one bite, maybe two
Would the citizens of New York be as empathetic
Toward a pure white ape & not bother
To rescue the overweight black 'dream girl'
Would beauty still have killed the beast

Synopsis

The girl on a voyage
                    is just
          a pretty face reaching
for an apple,
                    the kind of beauty
          he's looking for.

Neither beast nor man
                    can look away.
          Scream for your life.

Graven columns crumble,
                    released
          she crawls from the chasm.

He sniffs his fingertips
                    for her lingering scent
          & the damage has been done.

Hunting Kong: Supply List #1

Fay Wray's Scream Call

A revolutionary new fibreglass
horn features big volume screams
for long range calling. The detach-
able megaphone allows you to produce
realistic whimpers & other authentic
female-in-distress calls.
$99.99

Rigor Wray Doll

Kong won't be able to resist
the life-like quivering motion of
this life-size electronic Fay Wray doll.
Its realistic blonde hair & heaving
breast action is provided by a
dependable motor with a built-in-timer
decoy sequence of fifteen seconds on
& fifteen seconds off. A round base
allows for mounting almost anywhere.
$65.99

Déjà Vu

Walking around the *Exchange*
District. I hold sections torn out
from the yellow pages

> Antiques—Dlrs
> Book Dlrs—Used & Rare

I scour the streets entering sporadic shops.
Spotting anything *King Kong*—a toy, a postcard,
salt & pepper shakers, even an ashtray.

Browsing through books at *Borealis,*
the owner offers a *Flash Gordon* sign,
1934 , but that's not what I'm looking for.
Exploring *Toad Hall Toys,* I seek a model
for inspiration. I'm steadfast on *Kong*
(but could settle for *Godzilla,* at least he fought *Kong*).
To my dismay, the saleswoman suggests
the *Hulk,* an insult to my hero no less.

At *Aqua Books* I'm impressed with
a *Kong* fridge magnet, take it knowing
he'll soon invade every room in my house.
Ragpickers Anti-fashion Emporium & Books,
I pay for a paper *Plath* instead of the *King.*
Both colossus entities & timeless.

Hooper's Bazaar I spot my parents'
fish lamp & turquoise glass bar set.
Déjà Vu Antiques and More,
again, I come out notably nostalgic,
but empty-handed nevertheless.

While at *Red River Book Store* (digger's paradise)
I shuffle through piles of biographies
on the floor, then proceed to read
shelves sideways. The kink
in my neck growing stronger with each title.
On the other hand it could be worse,
a lady says, there could be mice!

My musty-smelling hands
still sliding in & out,
I surprisingly discover
The Creation of Dino De Laurentiis' King Kong.
With 'over 50 photos from the movie'
(the great ape remake) but not the copy
of *Fay Wray's* autobiography—
that's what I'm really looking for.

Someday I'll wish upon a star and wake up
Where the clouds are far behind me…

"Over the Rainbow" (from *The Wizard of Oz*)
Music by HAROLD ARLEN
Lyrics by E.Y. HARBURG

Misfits

My playwright husband
has written a script for me.
I thought he'd create
a more sophisticated role—
clearly we're not on the same page.

So, in the hot Nevada sun
I become Roslyn.
Rolled up blue jeans and boots
the blouse white
a symbol of purity
in my case naiveté.

The camera catches
my ass in the saddle
swaying to a whistle
or a song.

"I suddenly miss my mother," Roslyn says.
Arthur knows it's true—
knows I'm not acting.
Gay says, "I think you're the saddest
girl I ever met."
Arthur knows this too.

Arthur is my life, I used to say.
Now, I suffer through insomnia
anguish over absent children.
I swallow pills
drink down despair.
This is my drama.

Three cowboys round up
beautiful wild mustangs.
Not to break and ride—
but to slaughter for dog food.

Arthur keeps a notebook
not holding any flattering
words about me.
He's having an affair—
a pretty gal clutching her camera.

With each horse they subdue
my stomach becomes
a tighter knot.
The colt paws at its bound mother
and their screams echo through
the barren desert.

I howl hatred for the men
for their cruel killing.
Killing everything—
killing me.

Viewers believe I put on
a great performance—
in truth, I expose only half
the turmoil that rages in me.

This is the last scene—
Roslyn and Gay ride off
toward "that big star straight on."
Arthur and I start the shoot together
in the end, we depart
on separate planes.

This is my final scene
my last picture—
I die the following year
a misfit who knew
her lines well.

Starlet

everyone called me a dumb blonde
    yet I was neither blonde nor dumb

I read Chekhov, Tolstoy,
    Keats, & Shelley

took lit classes at UCLA
    Einstein & Lincoln my heroes

my hair a natural brown
    not platinum blonde

I was advised to bleach it out
    always doing what I was told

pose after pose—lean over, pout,
    undo this, take off that, put on this—

bathing suit after bathing suit
    seems I never had a choice

just a starlet with no direction
    didn't have control

maybe I never did
    as a child handed off to relatives

then left on the doorstep
    of an orphanage

rejected by everyone I ever knew
    married off at sixteen

never had real girl friends
    always jealous of my looks

thought I'd steal their boyfriends
    or husbands worse yet

well I learnt as a child
    men only want one thing from me

never gave me any respect
    yet controlled my life

but I could control the time I'd arrive
    on the set—leave them waiting

while I'd fret & fix myself
    or rather lose myself over—

to what they wanted me to be
    a calendar girl hanging

on their locker door or pinned up
    in some guy's greasy garage

strutting my stuff in stilettos
    across the studio stage

my behind waving for all
    to snicker & joke

my lips painted ruby red
    parted just enough

enough so men could imagine pleasure
    yes, I controlled the number of pills

I'd take to get through that media mess
    sure, I'd sleep with a lot of men

married men too
    the reality is if I didn't

I wouldn't get the part—any part
    the fact of the matter is

I liked being wanted
    being loved for even a brief time

I liked the sex
    but I couldn't control

the montage of miscarriages
    maybe if I'd been a mother

that would have changed
    people's opinion of me

my bosom would have become
    a symbol of nurturing

clean cuddling—not dirty sex
    I would have been a great mother

I loved children & animals
    I loved life

until I realized life didn't love me
    people would never see past

my naked body—
    see into my loving heart

so, in the end all I had
    was a stripped down naked life

nakedness everywhere

The Dress

The Dress is pure poetry
        its sunburst pleat & tapered folds
metaphors of a natural waistline
        that mid-calf hem—hand sewn
a cover up for something else going on
        is The Dress the object
or the woman wearing it?

The way her skirt floats above
        air pockets with a teasing tongue
lapping up the whistles
        scratching the itch of onlookers
the subway grate   still unmarked
        yet the woman remains
forever scarred

        A billowy ivory
        A halter bodice
        A tiny bow

tied together like a simile
more than a cardboard image
the soft fabric of a star's life
pressed for eternity

reflection

you sit on the bed
Norma Jeane's reflection in the mirror
black mascara drips to the clean slip
your mind spins its wheels
s c r e e c h i n g
"useless" "loveless"
invisible as the sun
on that haze-filled August day

how will you do it?
you have a distaste for blood
turns you nauseous
razor red wrists won't do

booze in your belly
eats a hole in your head
where you seep out
beneath your satin skin
crawling this way & that
flopping around in the dark

just go ahead & do it
s c a t t e r yourself off a bridge
let flowing water adopt you
miles from Hollywood, the hot sun
reflecting off your barren body
as you float past
barely visible through dark
sunglasses on blank faces
cameras snapping
one last shot

but you're in bed
all those telephone calls
stalling
in the end
dream your way with drugs
to heaven
the father you never knew
the sane mother
you craved

Growing Old

My mother turned ninety
born June 1, 1926
the same day as Norma Jeane—
who managed to morph
into Marilyn Monroe.

With the progress of time
mom now has many wrinkles
she's gathered a few pounds
but still looks pretty sharp
for a woman of her age.

If Marilyn were alive today
would she have aged so well?
I imagine she perhaps would have
sought cosmetic surgery of some sort.

As with the change of name
her transformation to Marilyn
not only included bleached blonde
hair, but also a new nose.

In this photo taken just after
World War II, my mother looks like
a movie star—like Marilyn.
Her long blonde hair curled just right.
Her lips, her teeth, her smile—
I can almost hear her laughter.

Marilyn always said
she didn't want to grow old
and she didn't.
Mom wasn't so vain—
aged with grace. Yet,
if they had met—
they would have hit it off.

Oh, Stell, you're too modest
Marilyn would say,
*You need to let yourself go
once in a while,
live a little!*
My mother would laugh
and reply *probably.*

Loving Groucho Marx

His thin build
lanky
His eyeglasses
thick
His brows & moustache
bushy

His silence often
He is my Father

That nose, that suit
      Your Dad could pass
            for Groucho Marx!
This is true
back in '75
in Laughlin, Nevada
my parents travelling

My Father is followed
          autographs sought
          along their walk
          photos snapped

My Father replies
      "No, I'm not him"

They laugh
continue their pursuit

He is clever
He is funny
He is dashing
He is silent

My Father Groucho
My Mother Marilyn
My life a movie

Houdini

Hanging
by your heels
hats a drift below
a death defying
dangle
suspended thirty feet above
for publicity's sake.

Winter in Winnipeg
frozen onlookers perplexed
that's free press for ya
photographers in awe
as thousands watch
beneath you banks piled high
there's a chill
and it's not only the weather
and you're not a dime museum act.

Out here in the prairie snow
straitjacket secure
you escape to the Orpheum
your audience awaits
a Foote in the door
at lightning speed your freedom

eclipse eight decades
like magic
you're in cyber space.

Motion Picture

1933—Ten-year-old girl

We stand beneath the marquee
look through the massive glass
of the theatre doors. People crowd
around a man, they are shaking
his hand. They are smiling.
The man is not. I ask my mother
who the man with the stone
face & funny moustache is?
My mother whispers *Herr Hitler*.
We make our way through the sea of red
velvet seats, sit in the last row against
the wall. *King Kong* roars on the big screen.
I watch the back of the man's head
more than I watch the movie itself.

2006—Eighty-two-year-old woman

Fragments of that earlier time
with my mother in the theatre
the smell of buttered popcorn eddying.
Now, *Peter Jackson's King Kong* is on CBC
Kong is about to be captured
taken away from his home
taken to the unknown.
He has fallen to his knees in the water
arms outstretched as he looks at his captors
with fear. I watch in disbelief as canisters
of toxic gas release fumes sedating Kong.
A queasy sickness begins in my stomach.
I remember the man with the moustache
the hard tug & pull of my mother's hand.

Star Wars

A long time ago
in a theatre far, far away
sat a young girl
newly wed

She knew nothing of marriage,
the Resistance or the Death Star,
Rebels, Jedi, or Ewoks
for that matter

But she watched
and learned
The text crawl
made her ponder

Princess Leia & Han Solo's
love became real to her
She discovered the dark side
and *may the Force be with you*

Forty years later
she watches a sequel
awakens again
to the mystery of that universe

Sure, the girl has aged
but so have Leia & Han
Now her grandchildren watch
Rey the heroine sporting goggles

Yes, the young will take over
the old will fall away
& in the final scene

the stars will shine
the planets will rotate
and a new hope awakens

For my part I know nothing with any certainty,
but the sight of the stars makes me dream.

—Vincent van Gogh

Superstar

Frida, can you see
the artist you've become
how you can't fade

& the blue house—still
stands in Mexico City
with all your votive paintings

Yet, they couldn't summon enough saints
to restore your broken column
or mend that artery of severed love

You were a faithful flower
a Rose, a red Rose—
Diego, a large wild Dahlia

overshadowing you
He became the star artist
but in the end, you outshine

Your Mexican roots run deep
just as wounds & scars
keep you from sleep

In the four-poster bed, you lie
propped with easel & brush
Tequila & cigarettes

another self-portrait of a superstar
Bird of Paradise—
threaded through your crown

You paint a thick brow & ominous eyes
homage to your life   a miscarriage unjust
everything for Diego

Why can you not see
beyond that marriage portrait
a revolution   you crop your hair

isolate yourself from the universe
but a star can shine
millions of years

The Starry Night, 1889 Vincent van Gogh
Oil on canvas

I set my easel
outdoors
on a southern summer
night

A starry royal blue
sky
lanterns glow a crescent
moon

The cypress stands almost
black
yet I know it is green layers
thick

Night swirls around
voices
within my head
halo

Shutters are closing
farewell to dawn's
madness

Church steeple
distant
beyond my reach

Teenager Buys Renoir Oil Painting for 35 Dollars

Neither a grainy reproduction nor *The Umbrellas 1886*
that still hangs in a London gallery, but a lesser-than,
a billion-dollar original, you painted after the first.
Nevertheless, I do believe you should be rolling in your grave
at such an irony. Your only depiction of a street scene—its sedate
linearity, half & half state—surfaced at a street emporium
in the US of A, bought for a meagre thirty-five dollars.
Now advertised for public auction it could sell for 3.5 million.

In Paris you couldn't persuade enough pretty women
to model for your gaiety. Two years after you began,
Aline, your wife-to-be, poses as the peasant woman.
Her umbrella & bonnet visibly absent, hands clutching the creases
of her skirt, your painter's eye reflects her sombre flawless face.
A tangle of hands—years later yours, too—would become twisted
& puckered with pain unable to flow with the brush.
You began *Umbrellas* disillusioned—impressionism fades
from your palette—strokes on the canvas a pervasive presence
of black & splashes of dark blue. A snapshot of purity
& grandeur on a crowded street wet with French tradition.

Before & after, light & dark. Not landscape—
or scene; *Monet Painting in His Garden at Argenteuil, 1873*
nor *Luncheon of the Boating Party, 1881.*
It's not a portrait; *Nude in the Sunlight, 1876*
nor *The Bathers, 1887*—for a mother would not have considered
the latter two a suitable acquisition for a teenage son.
Gone for a century—even now—this your last unfound
Beauty remains timeless & unwavering.

The Birth of Venus, 1486 Sandro Botticelli
Tempera on canvas

I stand beneath your feet
no pen nor paper
my mouth ajar with awe

From the womb
of the sea
birth of all births

Your bashful beauty
you rise it seems
shamed before you dawn

They came dancing
with cloth to cloak
shroud the sin of splendour

If words you did speak
they'd be pure poetry
floating on nymph wings

Those words would fall
from your parted lips
like petals of pink flowers

Like folds of fabric
ripples of shell
& shoreline

Untie your hair
open your arms
embrace your immortal reference

Waves of hair
waves of water
wash away sins

Ode to the Pomegranate

Oh, fertility Goddess of fruit,
in Mediterranean gardens you flourish
dark-green leaves lance-shaped, vermilion
flowers. Persephone's lust, leathery pink
skin envelopes ruby jewels
awaiting touch.

To peel your honeycomb with tenderness,
free you from your ivory bindings,
savour every succulent seed,
twirling each translucent capsule
on my tongue—smooth & perfect,
crunch your inner core between teeth.

Images preserved in Egyptian art,
your beauty—exquisite,
six hundred & thirteen—glittering rubies,
the number of commandments in the Torah.
Surely it was you Eve plucked
from the tree.

I count you.
Simmer you to jelly for toast,
toss you in a salad, & sip you in my tea.
Fasten you to a wreath
with eucalyptus & bay leaves,
hang you as emblem on my door.

Cobalt

I picture them cobalt blue
& when I'm feeling melancholy
I look to the night sky
to those stars
that somehow comfort me
wash over me
enable me to imagine
to dream to forget
the sparkle of a star
a softness
so delicate
like time
I'm drawn to cobalt
like a magnet
yet it's aluminum oxide
not nickel

I have spent far more than a nickel
collecting trinkets of blue
ink wells sea glass
vintage blue bird figurines
a Bohemian glass perfume bottle
I bought in Prague
there's the cobalt glass pitcher
rescued from a relative's garage sale
& the fashion—the shoes sweaters
& the coat

Ah the coat I can't forget the coat
1990's fitted & flattering
as blue as a Steller's jay
I proudly wore it to college class
time running out & late
a meager bowl of thick pea soup
toppled off the tray
supper all the way down the front
of that wool coat
I tried to no avail
to sop up the soup's
green mess dry cleaning
only managed to embed
this poem into fabric fibers
like an umbilical cord
thread of my past

Today blue lights trim my house
eliminate the red and green
consumerism of Santa's workshop
that once adorned the front porch
blue puts angelic back in the blessed season
brings Jesus home for Christmas
we're hopeful peace will come
I sit & sip hot tea
my *Moonlight Rose* teacup
its calming blue encircles
my thoughts again
return to that starry sky

Cementerio: Havana Cuba

Beneath a tangerine sun
Castro prepares his tomb—
envisions Lazarus
rising from the grave.
Hidden among angels & saints
in this perpetual
necropolis of crossroads
trees sway & sing
to the abandoned dead.

Removed from Revolution
Square—under a cloth-draped obelisk
bone, flesh eroded—
encased in cold white marble.
Statues of Jesus & the Virgin Mary
adorned with laurel—
execute a vigil over Castro's
perishing apotheosis.

Here he seeks catacombs of solace—
"La Milagrosa" protector of children
with Babe in arms—
Gracias Amelia chiselled into
tablets of stone here
she waits for Fidel to pass
beyond faith, hope, & charity
gateways to salvation
free him from his sins—
summon his bone-yard pantheons.

"Barbara Walters Goes Behind the Scenes
of the Revolutionary Surgery"
—ABC News

Mirror on the Wall

I watched Barbara Walters last Sunday night.
The woman with the first face transplant
made an appearance.
"I have a face like everyone else," she declared.
It occurred to me that she doesn't and that it was
an odd thing for her to say. The fact is that she
has a face like no other, the first of its kind, resembling
the tightly sewn face of a rag doll I once made.

The void in the story intrigued me. A piece
in this journalistic puzzle was definitely missing.
It became apparent to me that the dead dog
was the hero in this story & not the doctors
who performed the transplant. The Labrador
Retriever had tried to save his companion.
The woman had swallowed a fistful of sleeping pills,
passed out, & her pet tried in vain to retrieve
the pills she had ingested, tenderly, without malicious
intent, tore at her mouth, nose, & chin.

The woman intended to take her own life, but took
her dog's instead. Now euthanized, for mauling her,
his silence will prevail. The woman,
the proud owner of a new face, transplanted,
as fate would have it, from a beating heart donor,
who was also trying to commit suicide,

but didn't have a Retriever to save her life.
Both women wanted to die.
Both women, in some fragmented
persona of their former selves, live on.

Barbara Walters never asked about the sleeping pills.
Never asked the woman about her dog or if her face
was saliva-soaked before he tore it off.
Barbara only asked about the new face & the possibility
of it smiling soon.

Only that day dawns to which we are awake. There is more day to dawn. The sun is but a morning star.

—Henry David Thoreau

Sunshine

I watch the wasp
            drowning in my glass
of orange juice

Wings now sodden
            with nectar
he paddles the sphere in vain

Persists with the hope
            of emerging rejuvenated
& ready to take a bite from my arm

leave it red & swollen
            throbbing in pain
but today instead I will

watch him drown
            (it takes longer than I thought)
to sink to the bottom

sunshine upon
            his yellow stripes
in this sweet warm grave

Stargazing

like birdwatching

      searching

            for something

small

patient

specific

           sometimes

squinting

      telescope
      binoculars

          one

eye

        maybe

two

The Sun Is Also a Star

When I was a child
I sang *Twinkle, Twinkle, Little Star*
but oddly I can't remember
being outside after dark to have a firsthand look
at the stars in the night sky
I believe, I did possibly see them

When I was in my early teens
but I can't say for sure just when
I did watch them through my window
and the darkness of the country
made a sky full of stars
as I lay in bed waiting for sleep

When I was a child
I'd wish upon a star
wish to spend more time with them
learn their patterns in the night sky
the Big and Little Dipper and Orion with his belt
but, then again, the sun is also a star
and I spent hours basking in its daytime rays
my leopard print bathing suit
my skin lathered in lotion
my yellow Lloyd's transistor radio
me singing along to *Rocket Man* and *American Pie*
the heat of the 70's sun beating on my back
some days I'd wear a floppy hat
mowing grass while riding the tractor
pulling weeds in the garden
or picking raspberries in the patch

When I was a child
my Mother sang *You Are My Sunshine*
and if she could turn back time
I'd be that child again
and we just might slip out that window
together to gaze up at the Milky Way

Stars (Haiku #1)

Stars shine in night skies
Bright and twinkling as childhood
We know it won't last

Childhood (Haiku #2)

We wish upon stars
Our hopes just childish daydreams
Soon to be broken

Evening Star

I remember stars
filling the night sky
the chirp of crickets
the watery croak of frogs
I lay in the damp grass or on the hood
of a car or maybe even the roof
of the shed or the house
if I was really brave

On a clear night
star-speckled like a painting
as far as one could see
almost touching tops of trees
& the odd shooting star
or even a satellite
might pass by
if you were lucky

So peaceful in this country
no car horns or buses, no skyglow
just the shimmer of stars
the softness of nature
the rustle of leaves
or the coyote's cry
it too has a calming effect

Then in winter the crunch
of snow under my boots
the hoot of an owl
moonlight glistening
upon the white wrapped road
& there above in this starry night
is Venus and her familiar beauty
watching me walk the earth

Ode to Friends

For the friends we've lost
    along the way
the hours the years
    we've accumulated
on this naked prairie
    where we bared our souls
shared secrets we'd kept

For the risks we took
    that we'd later regret
For the tears we shed
    like clothes, that first time
& held each other after

For the drinks we drank
    in fields & barns
in the back seats of cars

For the times you held back
    my hair, wiped my face
For the dances we danced
    & the parties we crashed
For Pink Floyd & Zeppelin
    late into the night
For the smokes & gin we shared
    & promises we broke
For the moon on the white crust of snow
    & our breath hanging
frozen in the air

For the notes we wrote
    the hang-ups & door slams
arguments we later took back

For the late-night walks
    & early morning talks
For the times we wished we had
    & the times we'd wish we hadn't
For all the friends we've lost
    & will never get back

Starlite Drive-In

in those days, it stood so tall
like a monument stuck out there
on a large pie-shaped lot
over the other side of the tracks
far out in Transcona
the Starlite, with its shiny silver armour
reflecting the setting sun
as it hit its sleek back
while cars lined the long gravel entrance
their occupants waiting in anticipation
for the Saturday night darkness
& the double feature to roll
the trick was not to park too close
to the front of the screen
but not too far back
just a few rows ahead of the concession stand
but off to one side so its lights
& its noise wouldn't interfere
with our own little sound box
hooked on the window

but even then, the crackle
of the speaker would override
the movie sound & the characters'
voices would cut in & out
excitement overtook this inconvenience
as soon as the dancing hot dog
popping machine, or fountain drinks
showed up on the big screen
signalling refreshments were ready

car doors started opening & closing
lineups ran long for restrooms
the landscape of this parking lot a sea
of vehicles, every colour, shape, & size
cars, trucks, vans, & station wagons
by the time the second show started
windows were getting steamy
& back seats were full of the brave
if you needed a break you could walk
out among the rows of cars & hear
all the other speakers under the stars

Star Grill

Sun Rise

Mornings and afternoons
it might be about the food
the Cosmic breakfast
sounds divine had I risen
and ventured down Portage Avenue
for an early morning meal.

The Star Salad
tomatoes, cucumber, red onion
oranges & almonds
drizzled with a vinaigrette
perhaps a Rising Star, a Shining Star
a Shooting Star or a Heaven Burger.

Sun Set

The best time at the Grill is evening
tonight, tiny twinkling lights
offer an angelic ambiance
pairing perfectly with white wine
and my tarot reading.

The cards laid out on the table
he begins to map my constellations
in his monotone sure voice
past, present, & future
this radiant palate before me
my galaxy to explore.

House of Cards

In the tarot, the death card
could be the death of an idea
A headline disguised as an obituary
appears in the newspaper
Sears pulling the plug
at sixty-five years of age
after leading a vibrant and full life
ending an era for the retailer
a hard and determined worker
enjoyed the company of customers
touched the lives of many
families and employees alike
left suddenly in shock and grieving

The cherished estate
greedily fought over
by browsing bargain hunters
transformed into vultures picking
through the vulgar goods
who for the last few
decades were absent
from a decaying life

When sickness came
they failed to visit
but came for the funeral
to gawk at the empty
naked shelves and absent aisles
shamelessly left behind

Tarot Reading: XVI The Tower

Perhaps it's not as bad as it looks
but I'm no fool; I know disaster when I see it
Take a castle high on a rock—
solid—untouchable
not the storm rising
nor fires of hell reaching
can destroy it

Nevertheless, lightning bolts crash
splitting the tower in two
stone walls built to withstand
sudden change
The lightning is not a straight path
appears to have changed its mind—
wavered—toward another resolution

My head is not naked—I wear my crown
there is no absolute rule
Was there thunder I chose not to hear?
The windows bare
no curtains to hide the shame
fire has consumed them

Everything thrust out in the open
internal to external
Heaven exposed to the chaos of Hell
a gust of wind fans the flames
Perhaps I jumped and you fell—
& we scatter our separate ways

Stella

At eighty-five
my mother
began reading
fiction.

I had never before
in my time
seen her turn
pages of a real book.

Her recipe for life—
baking & cooking
and we gratefully
devoured it.

Now she enjoys
murder & suspense,
Mary Higgins Clark
or Agatha Christie.

Strangely, age
only mushroomed
this craving for more
books please!

At ninety her eyesight
fails, becomes a blur,
often falling asleep
with a book on her lap.

I bring a mystery,
read a passage,
softly turn pages,
watch her nod.

Time on Her Hands

A lifetime of washing dishes
first as the eldest daughter

tending seven younger siblings
later a husband & two children

Her Ukrainian heritage demanded
she cook, dirty dishes became endless

& now, at eighty-seven
she earns her first dishwasher

a quiet stainless-steel model
She allows herself to just rinse & load

to save all the time she has
on her age-spotted hands

I remember her asking for one
back in the late seventies

Dad always said it was a waste
of water & only nurtured laziness

She never would have bought one
but it came with the apartment

where she now lives alone

Origins

the ride to Vita always early
early in the spring
early in the day
as my mother wanted
to arrive
before the sun rose
high above the blossoming apple tree
before her father
made his way to the garden
to dig fresh potatoes for dinner
pinch some dill
pull baby carrots from sandy soil

the long drive
the adventure of the highway
when the hawk hit the windshield
the screech of the tires
& my mother in sync
then twelve miles of gravel road
slowing to a crawl
as a large painted turtle crossed our path
I'd count the wild turkeys in the ditch
or cows out in the pasture

some trips we'd arrive unscathed
greeted by Baba & her homemade doughnuts
& stewed rhubarb
these times
I would hear my mother
speak Ukrainian with her mother
I would look at her with wonder
think I don't know *this mother*
with Baba & Gido she'd flow in & out
English to Ukrainian
Ukrainian to English
My father & brother
oblivious to the change

Hairstory

You know I could never part with you
Yes, at times I've turned my back to you
cut you like a doll

& certainly, over the years
you have caused me grief

The teasing (I endured)
            Hey curly, whatcha do—
            Put your finger in a light socket?

The straightening (I inflicted)
            My head on the ironing board
            H e a t—too close, burned my scalp!

The dye colours (I envied)
            Natalie Wood—raven-haired
            in *Splendor in the Grass*
            Audrey Hepburn—chocolate brunette
            in *Roman Holiday*

(both characters cut their hair
as a symbol of female freedom)

            not a rebel without a cause

Hair—you know I could never part with you
oh, I've tried Dippity Do, & braided you too

Now I want you—*au naturel*—
let your curls fall where they may

Like Sophia Loren—auburn & wind-tossed
in *Legend of the Lost*

I admit I've weakened in my years
covering your grey for a shade of youth

Elizabeth Taylor—also raven-haired
in *A Place in the Sun*—still dyed at seventy-nine

Ah, but you'll be glad to know
I've decided not to imitate
Grandmother (God bless her soul)

Her bunned curls—dark auburn—
as she lay in her casket
a youthful eighty-two

Not me, no, I'll be cremated
waves of curls, the colour of ash

Child's Play

I dream of my pretend house
I'm maybe eight or nine
clear a pathway
through the bushes
create tiny rooms
line them with sticks & twigs
sweep my imaginary linoleum floor
with willow branches
I use an old rusty tobacco tin
stir juniper berries acorns
dry butterfly wings & seeds
make a bed of maple & poplar leaves
lay my head on a mossy pillow
look up through
tree tops   listen
watch clouds weave through
shimmering leaves
while chickadees & sparrows
chit-chat on my swaying roof
then I'd make believe it was dark
& the stars in the heavens were my nightlight
guiding me through my tiny rooms
I loved tending that house of mine
if only the work
of adulthood were that simple
& could be done outdoors
we'd store the innocence
of our childhood
in more than just our dreams

Shelterbelt

Amidst morning birdsong
to capture all the light of day

In spring, when sun thawed the ground
we plant thousands of seedlings

Ordered when snow sat on soil
from Indian Head, Saskatchewan

We map our Manitoba shelterbelt
imagine the sun reflecting its array of colour

Caragana & Colorado Blue Spruce,
Green Ash & Silverleaf Willow

My father measures
& digs the spaced holes

My brother places
& packs the plant

Trailer hooked to tractor
forty-five-gallon drums of water

My pail & large ladle in hand
I wait to soak each tiny tree

It would take a few years of summer
heat & rain barrel watering

For them to stand tall against
the cold wind & drifts of our winter

To the Moon

I would travel to the moon
      with you

Explore new galaxies
      along the way

Sail over calm waters
      fly over rough seas

I would travel to the moon
      with you

Stumble over rocky coastlines
      gaze over mountain tops

Cross over bridges
      climb up or down stairs

I would travel to the moon
      with you

            any time you ask

In one of the stars I shall be living.
In one of them I shall be laughing.
And so it will be as if all the stars
were laughing when you look
at the sky at night.

—Antoine de Saint-Exupéry
The Little Prince

1 Corinthians 15:41 *The Holy Bible*. Authorized King James Version, Red-Letter Edition. c2001 p.746.

The Hank Williams' lines in "Lonesome" are sourced from:
"I'm So Lonesome I Could Cry "
Words and Music by Hank Williams
Copyright 1949 Sony/ATV Music Publishing LLC
Copyrights Renewed
All Rights Administered by Sony/ATV Music Publishing LLC, 424 Church Street, Suite 1200, Nashville, TN 37219
International Copyright Secured All Rights Reserved
Reprinted by Permission of Hal Leonard LLC

"The Ballad of Hank Williams" was based on information drawn from the book *Hank Williams: Snapshots from the Lost Highway* by Colin Escott and Kira Florita, Da Capo Press, 2001.

"Tears Dry" was inspired by Amy Winehouse's music recordings as well as the books *Amy Winehouse: The Biography* by Chas Newkey-Burden, John Blake Publishing, 2008 and *Amy, Amy, Amy: the Amy Winehouse Story* by Nick Johnstone, Omnibus Press, 2011 and *Amy, My Daughter* by Mitch Winehouse, ItBooks, 2012.

"Amy" is an erasure poem created from the article "Winehouse film's focus on artist, not trainwreck," by Jill Lawless, *The Associated Press* reprinted in the *Winnipeg Free Press* July 3, 2015.

"Serious Moonlight" —the title is a reference to David Bowie's September 14, 1983 Winnipeg, MB Serious Moonlight Tour concert.

"Popstar" was inspired by two articles: "Ready to Belieb, again: Why we should be proud Justin Bieber is Canadian" by Anne Donahue, *Globe and Mail*, November 13, 2015. "Sorry on Purpose: Will Justin Bieber's apologies be enough to lure listen to his new album?" by Victoria Ahearn, *Winnipeg Free Press*, November 14, 2015.

"Stardust" is an erasure poem created from the article "IN THE MUSIC INDUSTRY, DEATH IS NOT THE END Jessica Contrera, *The Washington Post* reprinted in the *Winnipeg Free Press* January 23, 2016 .

Permission to use Gwendolyn MacEwen's poetry provided by David MacKinnon on behalf of her family.

The poem "After Leonard Cohen's 'How to Speak Poetry'" was inspired by "How to Speak Poetry," by Leonard Cohen, *Stranger Music: Selected Poems and Songs,* McClelland & Stewart, 1993.

"In Memoriam" —the opening quatrain is an excerpt from "The Tower of Song" by Leonard Cohen, *Stranger Music: Selected Poems and Songs,* McClelland & Stewart, 1993 Leonard Cohen and Leonard Cohen Stranger Music, Inc., used by permission of The Wylie Agency.

"Hunting Kong Supply List #1" and "#2" are based on S.I.R. Warehouse Sports Store, Fall 2006 catalogue.

Bahrenburg, Bruce. *The Creation of Dino De Laurentiis' King Kong.* Pocket Books, 1976.

Goldner, Orville and George E. Turner. T*he Making of King Kong: The Story Behind a Film Classic.* Ballantine Books, 1975.

Wray, Fay. On the Other Hand: A Life Story. St. Martin's Press, 1988.

"Media Illusions" —the epigraph is taken from the original 1933 film version of *King Kong* produced by RKO, producers Merian C. Cooper and Ernest B. Schoedsack, executive producer David O. Selznick, screenplay by James A. Creelman and Ruth Rose.

The quote "Some day I'll wish upon a star and wake up/Where the clouds are far behind me..." OVER THE RAINBOW (from "The Wizard of Oz") Music by HAROLD ARLEN and Lyrics by E.Y. HARBURG © © 1938 (Renewed) METRO-GOLDWYN-MAYER INC. © 1939 (Renewed) EMI FEIST CATALOG INC. (Publishing) and ALFRED MUSIC (Print). All Rights Reserved. Used by Permission of Alfred Publishing, LLC.

The poems referencing Marilyn Monroe were inspired by various articles from *Life* and *Newsweek* magazines, the *Winnipeg Free Press* and the *Globe and Mail* as well as the following book: *Marilyn*, text by Gloria Steinem, photographs by George Barris, Henry Holt and Company, 1987.

"Houdini" was inspired by a photograph from the book *Imagining Winnipeg: History Through the Photographs of L.B.Foote,* by Esyllt W. Jones, University of Manitoba Press, 2012 p.83. Lewis Benjamin Foote (February 6, 1873 – April 22, 1957) was a Canadian photographer, best known for his black and white photographs of early Winnipeg, Manitoba.

Van Gogh, Vincent. "For my part I know nothing with any certainty, but the sight of the stars makes me dream." Quote taken from Wheldon, Keith — *Van Gogh*, Bison Books, 1989 p.91

Thoreau, Henry David. "Only that day dawns to which we are awake. There is more day to dawn. The sun is but a morning star." *Walden* By Henry David Thoreau, Dodd, Mead & Company, 1946, p291(quoted in Walden 291)

Saint-Exupéry, Antoine de. *The Little Prince.* Houghton Mifflin Harcourt, 2000.

Acknowledgements

"Tears Dry" was published in *Prairie Fire* 36.1 *Electric City* 2 in May 2015 and broadcast at the Thin Air: Winnipeg International Writers' Festival in March 2013.

"Saturday Matinee" was published in *I Found it at the Movies: An Anthology of Film Poems*, edited by Ruth Roach Pierson and Sue MacLeod (Guernica Editions, 2014).

"Starland" was published in *A/Cross Sections: New Manitoba Writing*, edited by Katherine Bitney and Andris Taskans (Manitoba Writers' Guild, 2007).

"Media Illusions" was published in *Room of One's Own* (Vol. 29) in April 2006.

"Shelterbelt" will be published in the upcoming 2018 anthology *Heartwood: Poems for the Love of Trees* (League of Canadian Poets).

Thank you to the editors of the above journals and anthologies where some of these poems in some version appeared.

I am indebted to the Winnipeg Arts Council and the Manitoba Arts Council for their financial support in the writing of this book.

I am grateful to my writers group: Luann Hiebert, Sandy Stechisen, and Gerry Wolfram who offered criticism and praise for a great many of these poems.

Thank you to the star-filled cast at Turnstone Press for launching this book into the universe. And to my editor, Kimmy Beach, for her advice, her diligence, and her sparkle.

To my awesome friends, and colleagues who ask, "How's the writing going?" (You know who you are.) A big thank you!

Heartfelt thanks go to my family for their love and encouragement, especially my daughters: Rheanna, Jessica, and Alyssa. I am truly blessed.

To my husband, David Elias, my shining star, with much love and gratitude.